The Birds and the Bees

by
Sue Baker

Published by
Child's Play (International) Ltd

Swindon   Bologna   New York

© M. Twinn 1990
Printed in Singapore
ISBN 0-85953-400-6

Reproduction

Every individual plant or animal grows, matures, fades and dies. Some in minutes, some over many years.

Reproduction is the way species survive.

Reproduction may be sexual or asexual.

Asexual reproduction

Some plants and animals are neither male nor female and have no sexual parts.
They reproduce asexually by splitting or budding.

These are the most simple and rapid types of reproduction.
Every plant or animal reproduced asexually is essentially the same as others of its species.

Splitting

Many plants and animals consist of a single cell.
Complex life forms consist of many cells.

Each cell contains a nucleus which controls its structure, growth and reproduction, and, in fact, everything to do with the cell.

An amoeba reproduces by splitting into two.

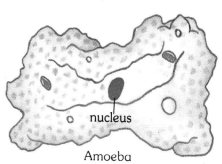

nucleus

Amoeba

First, the nucleus is duplicated.

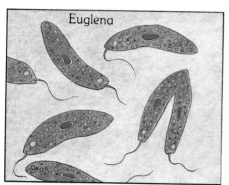

Euglena

Euglena divide lengthways. They are part plant and part animal.

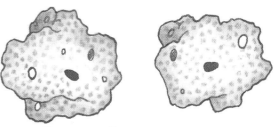

Two new cells replace the original.

We cannot say that one is the 'parent' and the other the 'offspring'.

Budding

Some multi-celled plants and animals reproduce asexually.
The Beadlet Anemone produces buds inside its body.
These develop into baby anemones
which it spits out through its mouth.

The baby plants are small replicas of the parent.
But we can see which is the parent
and which are the offspring.

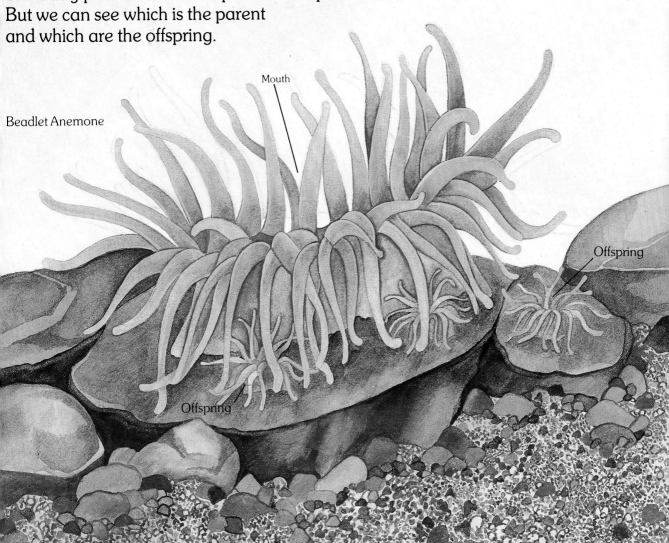

Mouth

Beadlet Anemone

Offspring

Offspring

Sexual Reproduction

Most plants and animals we know best reproduce sexually. Compared with species which reproduce asexually, this results in much greater variety in their offspring.

For sexual reproduction to take place, a male sex cell and a female sex cell unite. A male cell penetrates a female cell and fertilizes it.

Sexual reproduction in plants

In plants, female sex cells called ovules are contained in an ovary. Male sex cells called sperm are contained in pollen produced on the male sex organs, the anthers.

Fuchsia
♀♂

anther ♂

stigma ♀

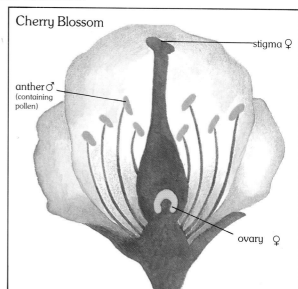

Cherry Blossom

stigma ♀

anther ♂
(containing pollen)

ovary ♀

Most plants have both male and female sexual organs, but most do not normally pollinate (fertilize) themselves.

Many plants depend on the wind or animals to carry pollen from one plant to another.

Birds and insects may be attracted to the plant to feed.
Pollen sticks to their body.
When they move to another plant, pollen is rubbed off again.

Hummingbird

wallowtail butterfly
n a Field Scabious

The fertilization of plants

When a pollen grain lands on the stigma, it grows a tube, which carries the sperm to the ovule. The sperm fertilizes the ovule.

This is the start of a seed, which grows into a new plant.

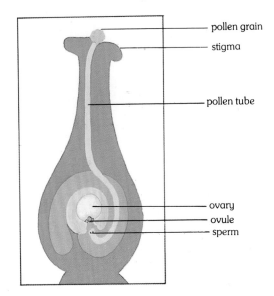

- pollen grain
- stigma
- pollen tube
- ovary
- ovule
- sperm

Seed dispersal

Seeds come in many shapes and sizes.
Seeds may be dispersed by wind,
water or animals.

Nuts and fruit contain seeds.

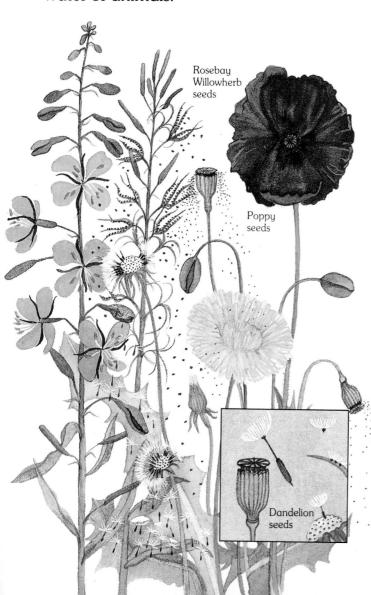

Rosebay
Willowherb
seeds

Poppy
seeds

Dandelion
seeds

apple pip

cherry stone

grape pip

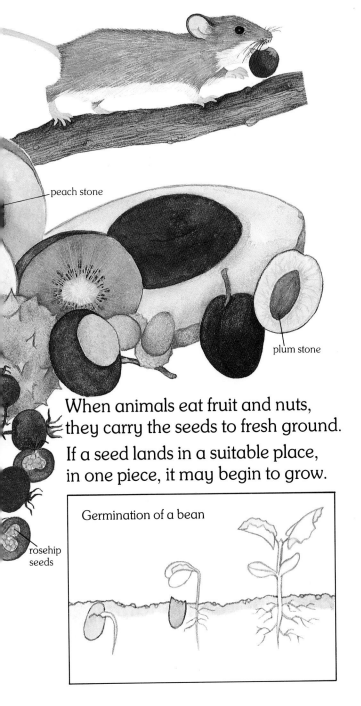

peach stone

plum stone

When animals eat fruit and nuts,
they carry the seeds to fresh ground.

If a seed lands in a suitable place,
in one piece, it may begin to grow.

rosehip seeds

Germination of a bean

Single sex plants

Some plants have only one sex.
They are either male or female.

They include kiwi,
poplar and juniper.

Single and dual sex animals

Some animals have both male
and female sexual organs.

But most of the animals we know best
are either male or female.

♀ ♂ ♀ ♂

Roman snails rear up and press the flat undersides
of their bodies together and caress each other
for several hours with their tentacles. At the height
of stimulation, they stab each other with a dart,
a signal perhaps for each to insert its male organ,
called a penis, into the other's female opening.

Fertilization in animals

In some species, fertilization takes place outside their bodies.

When frogs mate in water, the water carries the sperm to the female's eggs (frog spawn).

Common Frogs

♂

♀

Frog spawn

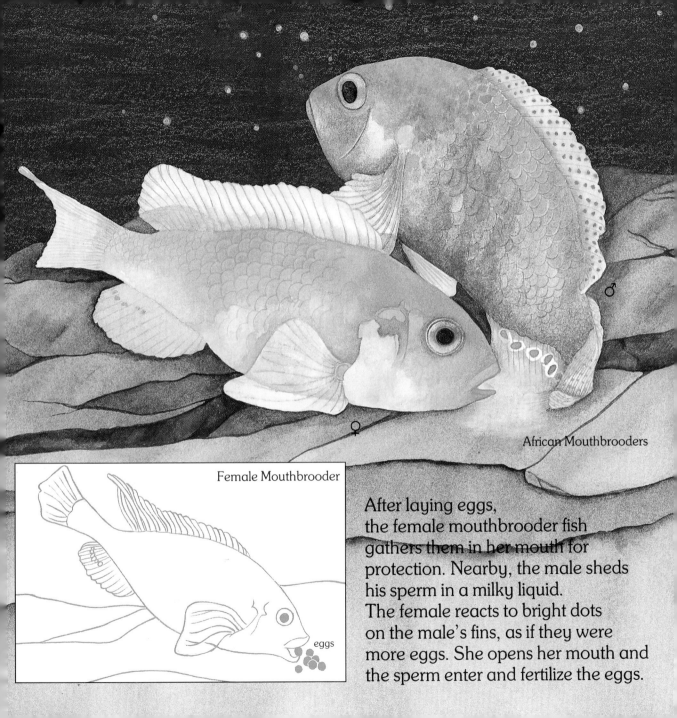

African Mouthbrooders

Female Mouthbrooder

eggs

After laying eggs,
the female mouthbrooder fish
gathers them in her mouth for
protection. Nearby, the male sheds
his sperm in a milky liquid.
The female reacts to bright dots
on the male's fins, as if they were
more eggs. She opens her mouth and
the sperm enter and fertilize the eggs.

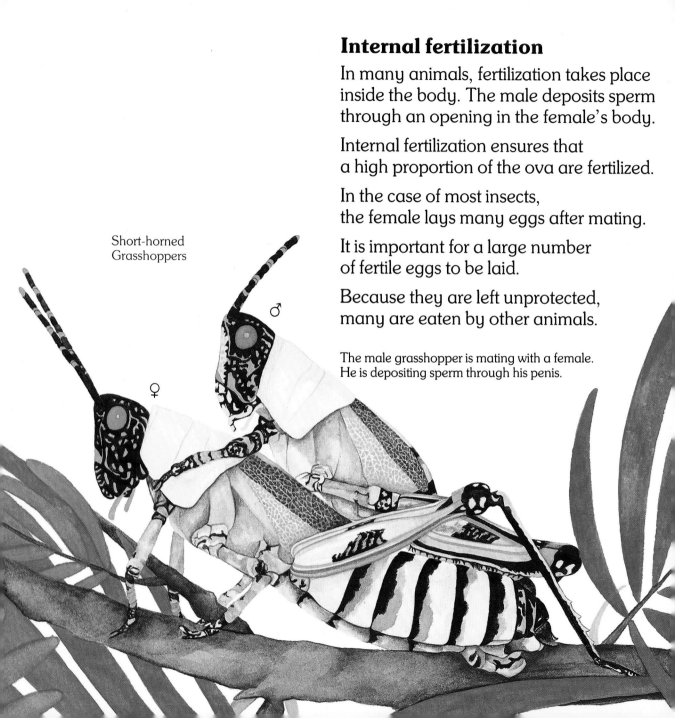

Internal fertilization

In many animals, fertilization takes place inside the body. The male deposits sperm through an opening in the female's body.

Internal fertilization ensures that a high proportion of the ova are fertilized.

In the case of most insects, the female lays many eggs after mating.

It is important for a large number of fertile eggs to be laid.

Because they are left unprotected, many are eaten by other animals.

The male grasshopper is mating with a female. He is depositing sperm through his penis.

Short-horned Grasshoppers

♂

♀

Development of young outside the body

Common Blue butterflies

♂

♀

single egg

These Common Blue butterflies are mating.

The female lays up to a hundred eggs, but only one on each leaf.

So, there will be plenty for the larva to eat when it hatches and it will be hard work for a predator to find all the eggs!

Count Raggis
Bird of Paradise

♂

♀

Attraction and courtship

In order to mate,
males and females of the same species
have to be attracted to each other.
Sound, smell, colour, dance, display
and other signals are used for attraction.

Many birds attract each other by song
and by rhythmic dance and flight.

Male birds are often more brightly coloured
than the female and attract a mate
by displaying their plumage.

Male frogs, such as this tree frog, call loudly to attract females.

Females can distinguish the call of males of the same species.

Tree Frog ♂

Male Baboon

penis

♀

♂

♂

Many females show signs that they are ready for mating.

The swollen rear of this female baboon announces that she is at her most fertile and arouses one of the dominant males.

Competition

Male animals often compete to establish superiority.
The strongest are the most likely to mate
and father healthy young.

Male mammals are able to father many offspring.
In many species, after mating, the male plays
no further role in the raising of young.

When animals live in herds or groups,
like these giraffes, the males compete for leadership.

The leading male may mate with many females.

Generally, there is less conflict
between females than males.

The number of offspring they can produce
is restricted by their breeding cycle
(how frequently they can become pregnant),
the length of gestation and how many young
they can carry.

As a trial of strength, male giraffes
push against each other with their necks.

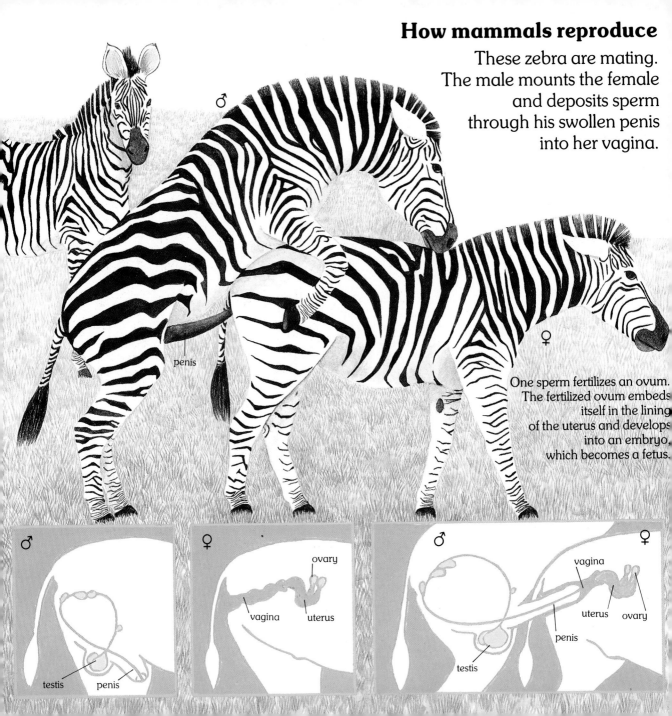

How mammals reproduce

These zebra are mating. The male mounts the female and deposits sperm through his swollen penis into her vagina.

♂

penis

♀

One sperm fertilizes an ovum. The fertilized ovum embeds itself in the lining of the uterus and develops into an embryo, which becomes a fetus.

♂

testis   penis

♀

ovary

vagina   uterus

♂

vagina

uterus   ovary

penis

testis

♀

Mammals are animals in which fertilization takes place internally and the young develop inside the mother. After they are born, they are fed with milk by the mother.

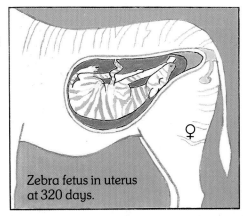

Zebra fetus in uterus at 320 days.

Gestation

The period during which baby mammals develop inside the mother is called gestation.

Gestation for a zebra lasts 350 days.

Birth of a zebra foal

Amniotic sac

teat

Zebra feeding her young.

Harvest mouse

Amazon parrots

Sexual maturity

Most plants and animals undergo a period of growth and development before they become sexually mature and are able to reproduce.

An elephant takes about 15 years. A parrot takes about two years. A mouse needs just 45 days.

For a species to survive, each member needs to be replaced by one mature healthy adult, during its life span. But to achieve this, there have to be sufficient offspring to compensate for infertility, drought, fighting, predators and disease. (And sufficient of each sex).

African elephants

Diversity

Sexual reproduction requires the union of a male and a female sex cell, each of which carries its own genetic imprint from the parent. (Genes determine every characteristic inherited by the offspring, such as how many limbs and their shape, and hair or eye colour). The result is a unique new individual. Although members of a species remain compatible, there are endless possibilities for variation.

Generally, it seems that diversity makes it easier to survive, to spread and to increase numbers.

Some characteristics are dominant. This can have advantages, such as adaptation to particular climates and situations and resistance to disease.

Farmers have used this to their advantage in order to breed plants and animals with particular qualities.

Building a home

The male stickleback changes colour to red
to attract a female and to let her know
he is ready to mate. He builds a nest.
When it is ready, he courts the female
with a complicated zig-zag dance.
He shows her the nest,
and as she swims through,
he prods the base of her tail.

She lays eggs in the nest.
Then the male swims through
the nest to shed his sperm
and fertilize the eggs
which hatch a few days later.

For some days, he stays
to protect the nest
and the young fish.

In this case, building
a nest ensures that
the eggs are fertilized.

♀

♂

The courtship dance
of the stickleback

The male prods
the female's tail.

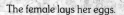
The female lays her eggs.

The male shows the female the nest.

Birds build a nest as a place of safety
in which to hatch eggs and rear their offspring.

It is easier to protect eggs and fledglings in a nest.
In many species, male and female birds
both take part in caring for their young.
They share in collecting food,
feeding the young birds, keeping them warm
and preparing them to become independent.

Blue tits

Social organization

Some animals, such as many species of ants and bees, are organized socially. It is a flexible and efficient system which has enabled them to survive for many millions of years.

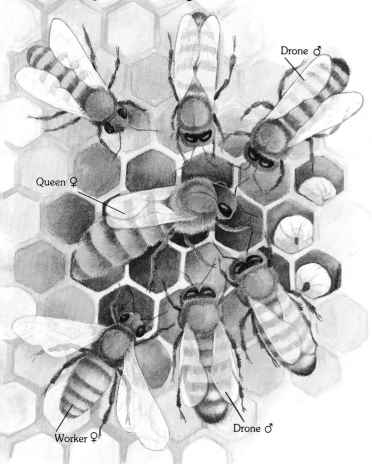

Drone ♂

Queen ♀

Worker ♀

Drone ♂

Each member has a specialized role and all work together for the well-being and survival of their society.

Most bees are female workers. They do not reproduce, but build hexagonal wax cells to store food in and for the larvae; they collect food (nectar and pollen); and they feed the larvae with secretions of food. These include 'royal jelly', which all larvae receive initially. This is rich in protein and continues to be fed to queen larvae, which grow bigger as a result. Larvae in worker or drone cells are fed with a nectar and pollen mixture (honey).

Male drones exist to fertilize a new queen. They live for only four or five weeks.

The queen's task is to lay eggs for the whole nest. After mating, she keeps sperm in a sperm sac, which fertilize the hundreds of eggs she lays each day.

Human reproduction

Human beings reproduce sexually. It is easy to tell the difference between boys and girls. Girls have a vagina. Boys have a penis and testicles.

Humans reach sexual maturity around the age of 12. Differences between sexes become more obvious. For example, boys grow hair on their faces and girls' breasts develop. We begin to use make-up, clothes, hairstyles, jewellery and perfume to attract. Even without these aids, our bodies are attractive in appearance and scent. We use our voice and body language. We desire to be close. We share music. We dance.

Competition

As we compete for a partner, we may become aggressive towards members of our own sex. Boys may fight over girls and girls over boys.

We may fight with our parents, too.
We may be unsettled by the changes
in our bodies, by emotional problems,
by lack of success. Parents may not
like the way we look and behave
or our choice of friends.

Courtship, love and marriage

But in the end,
even if we do not look or sound
like the persons we would like to be,
we find just the right partner.
We share ideas and interests,
we laugh at each other's jokes,
we are kind and thoughtful
and give each other presents.
When we argue or are apart,
we feel miserable.

When two people fall in love,
courtship may last for years.
In most societies, couples
usually pair for life.
This is often celebrated
by a marriage ceremony.

Building a home

Before we are ready to raise a family, we may want security, and to build a home. A place where babies will be safe and loved.

This is particularly important, because each female can bear few babies and children are dependent on their parents for a long time before they are sexually mature and even longer until they are ready to be socially independent.

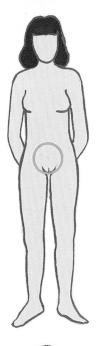

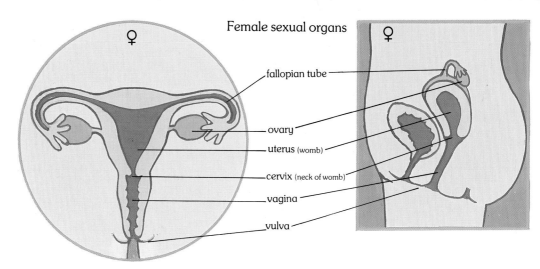

Female sexual organs

fallopian tube

ovary

uterus (womb)

cervix (neck of womb)

vagina

vulva

After reaching sexual maturity, girls are able to reproduce.
They usually release one ovum a month
from one of their ovaries.

Boys produce sperm in their testicles.

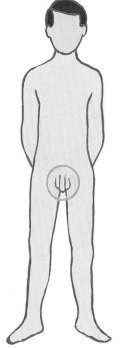

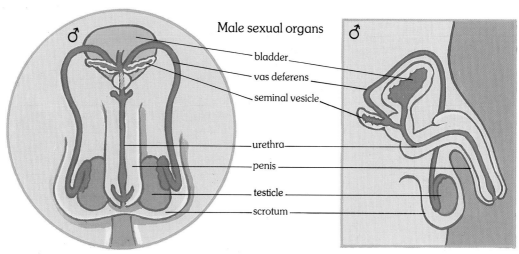

Male sexual organs

bladder

vas deferens

seminal vesicle

urethra

penis

testicle

scrotum

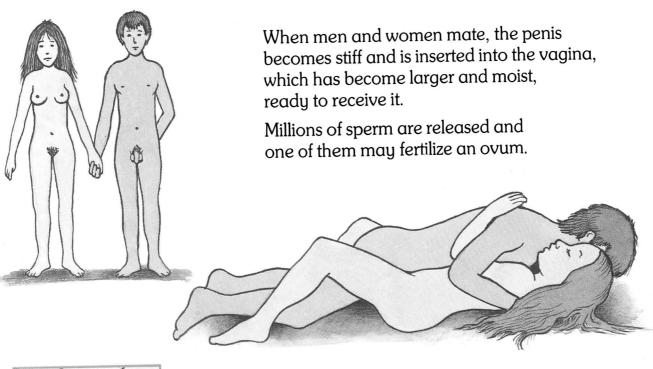

When men and women mate, the penis becomes stiff and is inserted into the vagina, which has become larger and moist, ready to receive it.

Millions of sperm are released and one of them may fertilize an ovum.

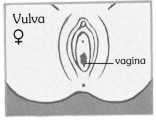

Vulva ♀

vagina

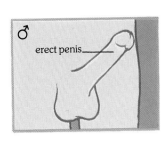

♂

erect penis

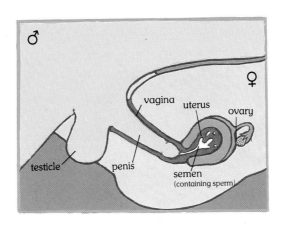

♂

♀

vagina uterus

ovary

testicle

penis

semen (containing sperm)

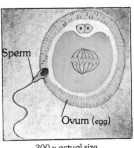

Fertilization

Sperm

Ovum (egg)

300 x actual size

Then, the fertilized ovum embeds itself in the lining of the uterus. . .
It will develop into an embryo and grow into a fetus.

Human beings are mammals

The gestation period of a baby is nine months.
After it is born, it is fed with milk
from its mother's breasts.

This is the start of a long period,
when the baby is dependent on its parents
for love and food, and to be kept warm and clean.